Secrets of Wing Chun

THE AUTHORS

Mr. K. T. Chao was born in Tientsin, China, in 1946. After schooling in Hong Kong he moved to Taiwan where he was awarded the LL. B. and the LL. M. degrees from N. C. U. He also holds the University of Oslo Certificate in International Relations and Peace Research. He attended the University of Cambridge, England, where he completed post graduate studies in law.

From the age of eleven Mr. Chao took an interest in Wing Chun Kung Fu. After mastering the Three Levels of Wing Chun, he became an instructor in Yip Man School and completed his study of the art. He is one of the leading experts of the Yip Man School. K. T. Chao's only Occidental pupil is the co-author of this book, J. E. Weakland.

Mr. J. E. Weakland, a Professor of History at Ball State University in Muncie, Indiana, U.S.A., received all of his degrees in America, including a Ph.D. from Case Western Reserve University. He was also a Fulbright Fellow at the Universities of Perugia and Rome, and a Visiting Scholar at St. Edmund's House, the University of Cambridge, England.

He is the author of a number of monographs and is on the editorial board of several journals. Mr. Weakland, who taught self defence techniques in the U.S. Army, has maintained a vital interest in the martial arts for over twenty years, an interest which is still very much alive today.

PREFACE

As practiced by the Shaolin Monks, Kung Fu was always used as a means of self defence and to protect the weak and enforce justice. It was an arcane art requiring considerable skill. When Kung Fu spread beyond the monastery, instructors continued to exercise great care in choosing pupils. Upright character and good behavior were of paramount importance. This situation has changed only recently. Today, thousands learn these fighting techniques, but with deplorable results. Quality has given place to quantity, and present instructors too often are lacking in knowledge and skill. As a result, they mislead their pupils, whether knowingly or not. The same is true, particularly so, of popular books and magazines which have appeared on the subject of Wing Chun. They contain little reference to or knowledge of the principles of the Grand Master, Yip Man, who passed away in 1973.

The purpose of this book is to discuss the origin, development, and secret techniques of Wing Chun. The principles behind the art are thoroughly analysed together with the movements. After perusing this book it should become clear that there is more to the art than one might assume after viewing modern popular "Kung Fu" films. It is more than a fighting technique. More properly, it could be called a way of life.

Secret Techniques

of

WING CHUN KUNG FU

(Sil Lim Tao)

Volume One

K.T. Chao & J. E. Weakland

Paul Crompton Ltd
London

1st edition 1976
2nd edition 1982
Reprinted 1997
3rd Edition 2014

All rights reserved

By the same authors:
Secret Techniques of Wing Chun Kung Fu (Vol Two)
(Chum Kil)
Secret Techniques of Wing Chun Kung Fu (Vol Three)
(Bil Jee)

ISBN 10: 0901764353
ISBN 13: 978-0901764355

Designed by Paul H. Crompton Ltd.
Photographed by I. S. Maclaren

Paul H. Crompton Ltd
94 Felsham Road
London SW15 1DQ

CONTENTS

ABOUT THE BOOK

In the East there has been a long master-pupil tradition. It is a tradition rich in wisdom, for one cannot reach perfection in any art without a teacher. Wing Chun has become increasingly popular in the last few years. Unfortunately there are few qualified instructors outside of Hong Kong, and those trained by Yip Man are even rarer.

This volume is not intended to be a sensational book in the popular vein. It is a reference work and a detailed and systematic instructional manual for serious students. The path to perfection in Chinese Boxing is narrow and steep. The training is rigorous, and the discipline is severe. We do not claim that this book can in any way be a substitute for personal instruction. But since personal instruction is not possible for most people, we do believe that this manual will enable diligent students to reach a high degree of skill, providing all the movements are practiced until they become instinctive.

This volume is devoted to the first level of Wing Chun which is called Sil Lim Tao. Although it means "little idea" or "little imagination", one should not disparage this level. For, it is the foundation upon which all else rests. Every major block, punch and strike is found in Sil Lim Tao. However, only when you know how to combine the basic movements of level one with the footwork of level two can you fight effectively. Yip Man used to claim that if a student had mastered the Sil Lim Tao techniques and the footwork of the second level and still lost a fight to a member of another school, then he, Yip Man, would leap from the roof of the Wing Chun School. Fortunately he never had to save face in that way because his students spread the fame of Master Yip and the Wing Chun system. In Hong Kong it was popularly known as the Lightning Hand School – an apt term indeed for this most subtle and scientific system.

In later volumes we intend to cover levels two and three, the 6½ point pole techniques, the construction and use of the wooden dummy, and the Wing Chun knives. These volumes will adhere to the format of the present edition. After each movement is analysed, individual exercises are presented. These are followed by sparring sets for practice and examples of self defence applications. The work ends with the complete Sil Lim Tao set.

Heeding the advice of the Chinese proverb that one picture is worth a thousand words, we have included abundant photographs for each movement.

Since there is little uniformity in transliteration, Chinese words have been kept to a minimum. The English term has been used with the Chinese word in parentheses.

It is said of the Tao: "Use it and it is inexhaustible." Do not just read this manual. Use it and you will discover that the secrets of Wing Chun are also inexhaustible.

HISTORY

Although Kung Fu is a term which refers to any skill, it has become popularly associated with Chinese boxing. The history of Kung Fu is so shrouded in legend that the truth will probably never be discerned. Rather than attempt an impossible critique, the traditional history of Wing Chun is mainly recounted.

The invention of Chinese boxing and its identification with the Shaolin Temple are usually attributed to Bodhidharma, founder of Ch'an Buddhism. In fact we do not know who instituted the Shaolin Temple, and it is highly questionable that Bodhidharma was responsible for even inchoate versions of Kung Fu. His book of exercise was not published until 1624 A.D., over one thousand years after his death. We do know that around A.D. 495 a temple was constructed in Honan. It was called "Shaolin", meaning "Young Forest", for only a young tree can survive the violence of wind and storm, because it bends and sways, whilst a "tree that is unbending is easily broken." This most famous of Buddhist temples had a remarkable capacity for survival. From the sixth century onwards it was destroyed and rebuilt many times. It was more like the fabled phoenix than a young tree.

Fighting techniques patterned after animal forms eventually became a basic part of a monastic discipline. Each of the five animal forms was designed to develop a different essence: the dragon (spirit), the tiger (bones), the leopard (power), the snake (breath), the crane (energy). Other movements were added through the course of centuries. Like the temple itself, the skills of the Shaolin priests became part of the mythic experience of ancient China.

After the fall of the Ming dynasty in the seventeenth century, the Shaolin temple became a centre for revolutionary activities against the hated Manchu Emperors. Even the traditional Shaolin greeting had a symbolic political meaning. The open left hand is placed over the closed right fist. The open left hand signifies the moon, whilst the clenched right fist denotes the sun. These characters in Chinese mean "Ming".

During these times the monks taught a number of lay people the art of fighting. Sensing the danger, in 1729 the Manchu Emperor passed a decree which prohibited the teaching of Kung Fu; but the Shaolin priests did not obey the decree. The forms were practiced in the dim light of the early morning hours. (In 1930 a visitor to a Shaolin temple observed that the monks practiced in the early morning because of this tradition dating back to the eighteenth century.) At first the Emperor decided to move indirectly against the monastery. In 1735 the Governor of Honan received a command concerning the demolition and reconstruction of the temple. After some remarks about suspected revolutionary activities in the province, the Emperor said that he had heard about the sad condition of the Shaolin temple and that it was badly in need of repair. Therefore he ordered the destruction of the old structure in order to build a new one. In front of the old temple were about twenty-five houses, a long distance from the shrine, behind which Kung Fu was practised. The organic structure of the temple made it difficult to control; thus the Emperor consolidated the buildings when he had the monastery rebuilt. Nevertheless a number of secret passages remained and the Manchus still feared the monks. At last the Emperor decided to destroy the temple, but the army could not breach its defences. When the monastery did finally fall, it was due to the traitor, Ma Ling Ër, a Shaolin monk turned renegade.

Ma Ling Ër had broken an ancient lamp, by accident, while cleaning it. Although he received the regular, though severe, monastic disciplinary measure for his carelessness, he felt that the punishment was unwarranted. His resentment festered into hatred and he left the temple and joined the Manchu army, offering his services to a high-ranking official named Chan Man Wai. Chan Man Wai was told the secret plans of the Shaolin complex by the treacherous Monk. The monastery was razed to the ground about the year 1768.

According to tradition there were only five survivors – henceforth called the Venerable Five of Shaolin. They were: Ng Mui, Pak Mee, Fung Do Tak, Miao Hin, Gee Sin. Since the traitor Ma Ling Ër had taught the traditional Shaolin movements to members of the Manchu army, the Venerable Five know that new techniques would have to be developed. Each of the Five had a speciality. Miao Hin excelled with knives. Gee Sin with sticks, etc. It was the Buddhist nun, Ng Mui who possessed the greatest boxing skills. The Venerable Five scattered. One settled on a mountain in Szechwan, another established a Shaolin temple in Fukien, a third lived on Wudang Mountain, while a fourth lead a peripatetic existence. Ng Mui found shelter on White Crane Mountain in a place called the Green Temple. There she met a young girl named Yim Wing Chun to whom she passed on the art of Kung Fu. Yim Wing Chun instructed her husband Leung Bok Cho. The knife techniques were transmitted to Wing Chun and her husband by Miao Tsui Hua, the daughter of Miao Hin. Then Leung Bok Cho taught Leung Lan Kwai, whose successor in turn was Wong Wah Bo, a member of an opera troupe. In the troupe was an actor named Leung Yee Tye and by a remarkable coincidence – perhaps not so remarkable in legends – there was a Gee Sin – one of the Venerable Five – disguised as a cook. Ge Sin trained Leung Yee Tye in fighting with sticks, i.e. the 6½ point pole techniques. Wong Wah Bo and Leung Yee Tye exchanged their knowledge. Thus it came to be that knives and sticks together with boxing became part of the Wing Chun system. Leung Yee Tye's successor was Leung Tsan, a gifted doctor who lived in Fatshan, a town in Kwangtun Province. Chan Wah Soon then followed. Although he taught Wing Chun for almost forty years, he had only sixteen selected students, one of whom was Yip Man.

Yip Man was from an aristocratic family in Fatshan. At the age of thirteen he began to study Wing Chun under Chan Wah Soon. The instruction continued for three years until the death of Chan Wah Soon. Shortly after, Yip Man went to Hong Kong to study at St. Stephen's College. While in Hong Kong he met Leung Tsan's eldest son, Leung Bik, who easily defeated Yip Man in a private contest. After that the young Yip Man learned many more techniques from Leung Bik. When Yip Man returned to Fatshan at the age of 24, he was a master of Wing Chan. His skills remained to the very end of his life. This great Grand Maser died in 1972, in Hong Kong, where he had settled in 1949. The world may never see another like him. He was the embodiment of a vanished civilization.

WING CHUN PRINCIPLES AND MAXIMS

Wing Chun is unique in many ways. Perhaps its greatest singularity lies in in the fact that it is the only Shaolin system to have been devised by a woman. For this reason Wing Chun is especially suitable for women. The system depends on technique rather than power. The force of Wing Chun is like that of a coiled spring when released, but without tension.

Normally, Kung Fu systems are divided into Northern and Southern schools. Wing Chun belongs to the latter. In the North there was a great deal of fighting from horseback in which the rider would use kicks to protect himself; the horse stance, so basic to all Kung Fu schools, developed as a result of this type of combat. In the Northern systems there are numerous high kicks, many of which are off to the side and the arm movements are long and wide. In general, Northern Kung Fu requires considerable strength and agility. In contrast, Southern styles like Wing Chun have few kicks; and the arm movements tend to be short and narrow. Relatively little space is required, and years ago demonstrations used to be given on large round tables. There are exceptions of course, but what has been stated certainly applies to Wing Chun. It is an excellent means of developing your body and keeping fit; however the execution of Wing Chun requires neither exceptional natural bodily strength nor sheer brute force. In this sense, Wing Chun is more an internal system stressing the development of refined force. There is a proverb of Wing Chun School: "Think of yourself with a glass head with a bean curd body protected by an iron hand." Yet, with paradoxical logic so typical of the East, another maxim states that in the horse stance the body is like a mountain from which the hands move like lightning.

It is the lightning quality of the hand and arm movements which characterizes each of the three Wing Chun forms or levels. The first form, Sil Lim Tao provides the basic training for all that follows. From a powerful and stationary horse stance all the fundamental hand and arm movements are practiced. As in all things it is quality rather than quantity that counts. Be patient. "Do not force things. It is dangerous to deviate from instructions or push for completion. It takes a long time to do a thing properly. Once you do something wrong, it may be too late to change" – Chuang Tzu.

The second level is called "searching for the bridge" or "arms seeking" (Chum Kil) and emphasis is placed on defensive techniques such as the low wing hand, kicks and turns. "Thrusting fingers" or "flying fingers" (Bil Jee) is the third and final form. As the name indicates, the fingers rather than the fists are the weapons. In addition, there are complex combinations in which elbows, palms and fingers are combined with rapid leg movements as one defends and attacks at the same time. On all levels attack is accentuated, and it is an attack in which there is no set pattern. On all levels, too, one blocks and hits simultaneously.

Although there is nothing mystical about Wing Chun, as in other Kung Fu systems, it incorporates the ancient Chinese philosophical principles of Yin and Yang with all of their paradoxes. The cosmology is based on the "Book of Changes" (1-Ching) which views the universe as one great unity – a unity of opposites. Yin is the dark half of the circle and represents the feminine and the negative, while Yang, the white half of the circle, symbolises the masculine and positive. Yet there is a small white circle in the black portion and a small black circle within the white sector.

Fig. 1.

The meaning: everything includes its opposite – unity is a balance of opposites. Strength is concealed in weakness and weakness is concealed in strength. One of the purposes of Chinese boxing is to "harmonize antagonistic movements both within oneself and in relation to an opponent."

Although the combat may be with an opponent, it can imply a spiritual struggle in which one resolves interior contradictions.

If Wing Chun becomes a part of your life, it can help you to achieve a greater harmony of mind and body. It will teach you to feel the present moment, which is so vital to mental health. Your mind will become more flowing as you begin to respond instinctively without thought of ego, without concern for victory or defeat. This is part of the long Shaolin tradition. "So then, flow with whatever may happen and let your mind be free: stay centred by accepting whatever you are doing. This is the ultimate," said Chuang Tzu. But such stillness can only be achieved with the help of another. You must work with a partner, who will be in fact your spiritual brother. Together you will attain discipline in spontaneity and spontaneity in discipline. A precept of Tai Chi Chuan is applicable to Wing Chun also: "From familiarity with the exercise there comes a gradual realization and understanding of force. From the understanding of force there comes a spiritual illumination. But it is only after long, diligent practice that this sudden seeing-through will be achieved." (Wang Chung-Yueh).

Secret Techniques
of
WING CHUN KUNG FU
(Sil Lim Tao)

Some Principles and Maxims of Wing Chun

THE FOLLOWING ARE SOME MISCELLANEOUS PRINCIPLES 7 MAXIMS IN WING CHUN:

1. Because of their deceptive appearance, monks and nuns, women and scholars are the most dangerous practitioners of Kung Fu.
2. The palm is Yin because it inflicts internal damage, but the fist is Yang for it causes external harm also.
3. A punch with the fist reaches farther than a strike with the palm.
4. The shortest is the most correct, i.e. straight line punches are the most effective. This is shown in Figs. 2, 3, 4.

2

3

4

Fig. 2. A top view of 'A' executing a right arrow against an opponent.

Fig. 3. Side view of 'A' executing a right arrow. Wing Chun punches travel along the centerline.

Fig. 4. This shows a man throwing a circular punch. It has further to travel. The punch from a Wing Chun man – see Fig. 3. – would arrive first.

5. When an opponent's hand goes out, search for his body and not his hand. See Figs. 5 and 6.

Fig. 5. The man on the left executes a wide block.

Fig. 6. The Wing Chun man on the right strikes to the opponent's body directly.

6. The Wing hand is the best or the worst of movements.

7. Never execute a Wing hand without a Protective hand, and move forward: but remember that the body follows the Wing hand forward.

Fig. 7. Side view of a Wing hand with Protective hand, and moving forward.

8. In fighting, the arrow punch is always delivered while moving forward.

Fig. 8. Side picture of an arrow punch while moving forward.

5

7

6

8

9. If he comes, let him stay, but if he moves, punch straight to the body. This is similar to maxim no. 5. In other words, when your opponent moves his hand away from your block in order to throw another punch, you should punch straight ahead and not follow his hand. Figs. 9 and 10.

Fig. 9. Side view of Wing Chun man blocking.

Fig. 10. Side view of Wing Chun man delivering a straight punch as his opponent moves his and away to deliver another punch.

10. In Wing Chun, you block and attack at the same time. Figs. 11, 12 and 13.

Fig. 11. Side indoor. The Wing Chun man is doing a left open hand block and a right arrow at the same time.

9

10

11

Figs. 12 and 13 show examples of another school in which one blocks first and then attacks.

11. When an opponent's forearm is coming, cross over it to punch.
12. When there is an opportunity to hit, then you should hit, but if your punch is blocked, then don't attempt to complete the blow improperly.
13. Don't be too anxious to hit; otherwise you will be hit.
14. Don't be afraid of being punched; otherwise you will be punched.
15. Like a snake in combat, always face your opponent directly, i.e. face your opponent's centreline.
16. If an opponent feints a punch, take it as a real punch; block it and attack at the same time.
17. Wing Chun fists and kicks are unseen by the opponent.
18. Prevent a kick with a kick.
19. Relaxation and speed are of the utmost importance in executing an effective punch.
20. Merely dodging punches by moving the body away as some schools advocate is not an efficient method because once you retreat, you must continue to retreat; and you cannot move as rapidly backwards to escape as your opponent can move forward to attack.

It is fitting perhaps to close this chapter with the regulations of Yip Man's school:

1. Keep the rules, and respect the fighting code.
2. Practice etiquette and justice; respect and love your country.
3. Love your fellow students at the school, and work for the solidarity of the group.
4. Be strict in matters of sex; make your body healthy.
5. Practice diligently, and never forget the techniques.
6. Be gentle and polite.
7. Help the small and weak; use the techniques to show benevolence.
8. Respect the heritage of the school.
9. "A good fighter is never angry." (Tao Te Ching)
10. "Great courage is not aggressive." (Chuang Tsu)

12

13

THE HORSE STANCE

Part One –
The Basic Position

The pigeon-toed stance of Wing Chun is also referred to as the "internal-rotated adduction stance". All Kung Fu systems make use of the horse-riding stance, an awkward looking position, but a great source of power, and flexibility. "Your feet are the root, the energy passes through your legs, control is in the waist, and form emerges in your hands and fingers" (Chang San-Feng). Wing Chun does not use such stances as the bow and arrow, the cat, the scissors, the charging horse, etc. Typical karate and boxing positions in which one leg is extended with weight on it are extremely vulnerable to kicking attacks. In Wing Chun there are three stances. A. the front stance, B. the side stance, and C. the changing stance. The latter two are only introduced at level two. In this volume we will only be concerned with the front stance, i.e. the bent-knee, pigeon-toed horse stance. Throughout the book this will be referred to as "the basic position". In level one you do not move from this position. The exercises, the sparring, and the Sil Lim Tao Set are all performed while remaining stationary in the horse stance. Sometimes you will see that the photographer has illustrated one movement from various angles. Keep in mind that the person doing the movement has not moved.

Fig. 14. Stand with your feet together, arms hanging loosely at sides. Empty your mind of extraneous thoughts. Breathe easily and naturally through the nose. Relax your body and allow shoulders to come forward.

Fig. 15. Bend knees and drop into a quarter squat position as if about to sit, torso held straight. Simultaneously raise your hands, clench fists and turn palm upwards while moving hands back to level of chest. Neither fists nor forearms should touch the body.

Entering Horse Stance

Fig. 16. Slide feet outward by pivoting on heals, but the soles of the feet should also slide and remain in contact with the floor. Note that the position of the feet forms an angle of about 180 degrees.

14

16

Fig. 17. Remember this is a front view of the basic position. To reach it shift your weight on to your toes and simultaneously slide your heels outward. Do not move the body from the quarter squat position. You are now in the basic, fists back, horse stance position. Some state that the toes should form a ninety-degree angle to each other. The angle is of less importance than the

fact that the knees are drawn close, pointing towards each other. This gives stability and flexibility. The centre of gravity of the body has now shifted to the lower part, i.e. between the knees. Yip Man used to tell his students to imagine that they were trying to trap a goat below their knees. The head is held erect, eyes looking straight ahead.

Fig. 18. The upper body leans slightly backwards, and the back is not arched. Viewed from the side the back of the head and the heels are in a perpendicular line.

One important training secret: keep the buttock muscles tensed while in the basic position. The horse stance thus becomes an isometric exercise which will help you develop enormous strength in your lower body. Needless to say, your horse stance will become powerful. In free sparring and actual self-defence situation, the buttocks are relaxed.

When Yip Man first came to Hong King he gave a remarkable public demonstration of the refined force which he developed after years of horse stance and Tan Tien training. Although he was quite small and already in his fifties, seven husky labourers were unable to move him, pulling on a rope tied to one of his legs when the other one was raised off the ground…

15

17

18

Part Two – The Front Fighting Stance

Assume the basic horse stance, extend one arm in front (left or right) with the other near your chest. The extended hand is known as the "inquisitive hand" (Man Sao) while the hand behind is called the "protective hand" (Wu Sao), acting as a rear guard. It does not matter which hand is extended and which held back. In free sparring and self defence you might change hand positions many times. The main point is that you face the centreline of your opponent (Jiue Ying). If your opponent is in a Wing Chun front stance with his right hand extended, then you would generally extend your right hand also; but this is not a rigid rule. Most of the time you will find yourself blocking your opponent's inquisitive hand. Study figures 19, 20 and 21 carefully. Observe your position in a mirror. In fact it is a good idea to do all of your individual training in front of a mirror.

Figs. 19/20. (19 shows front view, 20 the side). Note that the elbow of the inquisitive hand is about three inches from the body, with forearm and hand pointing toward the centreline of the body at about heart level. The protective hand is slightly away from the body in a "prayer" position with the palm on the centreline. Make sure that the protective hand, forearm, and elbow do not touch the body.

Fig. 21. This shows the top view. The man on the right is in the fighting stance, to show that you should face the centreline of an opponent.

19

20

21

Part Three –
Centreline Theory

The centreline or vertical mid-line theory (Joan Sien) is an essential part of Wing Chun. While defending your own centreline, you attack along the vertical mid-line of your opponent. The main weak points of the body are along this line. (See Fig. 22, showing main weak points of the head and eyes, nose, upper lip, throat and neck, heart, stomach, bladder, groin).

22

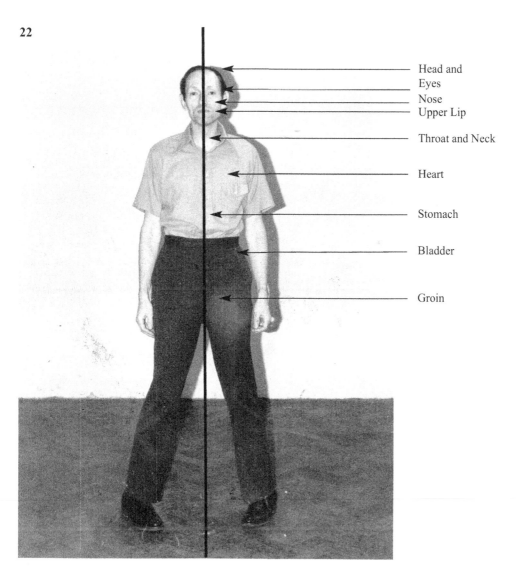

Head and
Eyes
Nose
Upper Lip

Throat and Neck

Heart

Stomach

Bladder

Groin

Figure 23 shows a front view of the centreline – high, middle and low areas.

In Wing Chun the body is divided into three defending areas: high – from head to solar plexus, middle – from solar plexus to groin, low – from groin to feet. The high and middle areas are protected by both arms. The low area is defended by co-ordinating hands, footwork and horse stance. Most of the defensive manoeuvres for the low area will be covered in another volume. The lines in Fig. 23 define the boundaries for the hand and arm movements. In blocking you never move your arms beyond your own indoor area. This will be explained later as each block is introduced, as will the use of the indoor and outdoor areas.

23

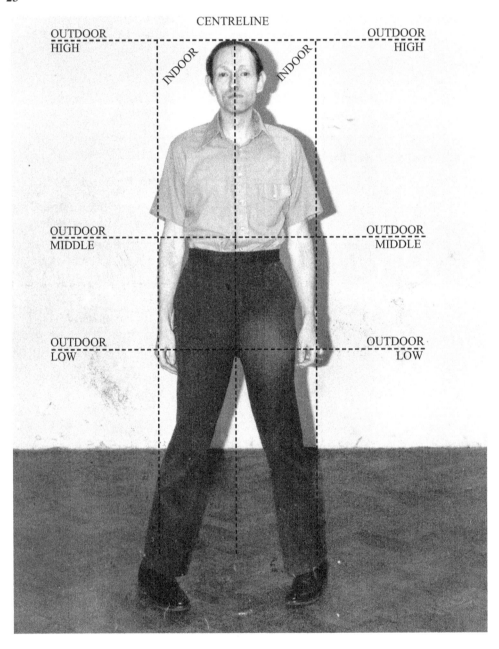

Wing Chun
Hand and Fist

Fig. 24 gives a close-up of the "leaf palm", the name given to the open hand in Wing Chun. The thumb is tucked in for protection. Figs. 25 and 26 show respectively the side and top view of the fist. The closed fist is like the ordinary boxing fist. Punches are delivered with the palm to the side and the wrist straight. Wing Chun punches can be delivered with various twists at the wrist, but these will only be introduced at level two. The ordinary vertical punch is effective enough without a twist.

Double Elbow Punch

Fig. 27 shows the arms extended in front, palms down. From basic position, extend the arms straight out, shoulder level, parallel to the floor, palms down. Fig. 28 shows the side view of the basic position. Return the arms back rapidly to the basic position while closing your fists and turning your palms upward. During this exercise concentrate on the elbows. Repeat for two sets of fifty repetitions. The application is obvious enough not to need an illustration. IF someone grabs you from behind, reply with a single or double elbow punch.

24

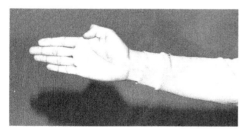

25

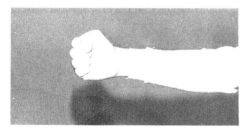

26

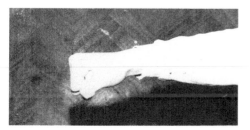

27   28

Double Cultivating Hand

Fig. 29 shows front view, left arm over right in front. From the basic position bring your arms down, while opening your hands to form the leaf palm. Palms face the body. At the completion of this downwards sweep the arms should be crossed at the wrist, with left over right.

29

Figs. 30/31. Raise your arms and then return to the basic position. Repeat for 25 repetitions. The application of the cultivating hand is discussed in a later section of this book. Normally the double cultivating hand movement is done in connection with a breathing exercise with we have not included in this volume.

31

30

THE ARROW PUNCH

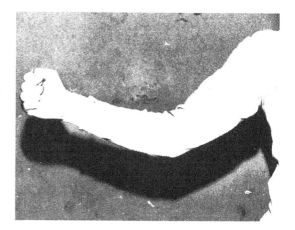

This most important of all Wing Chun punches is known by various names: arrow punch, straight punch and vertical fist. We prefer the term "arrow punch" because the position of the arms resembles drawing and releasing a bow. Yip Man placed a great deal of emphasis on this punch, and Mr. Chao's colleague the late Bruce Lee used to practise it daily for 500 repetitions each hand. The arrow punch is an excellent example of the directness, the straight line style of attack and the economy of movement which characterize Wing Chun. The power of the punch is dependent upon several factors.

1. The power generated at the shoulder and elbow joints.
2. The power of the extensor muscles of the arm – the triceps.
3. Speed of delivery.
4. Method of execution – elbow in, straight line punch along ht e vertical mid-line.

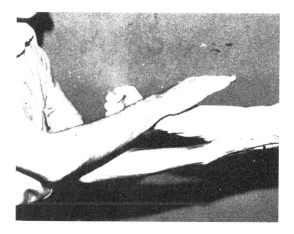

It must be a piston-like punch which can only be achieved when the elbow is relaxed. You must "crack the air" with the punch, but the shoulder joint must not come into play. Although the shoulder joint is obviously involved, the real power is generated at the elbow joint: therefore you must learn to relax your elbow. This applies before and after the punch. All Wing Chun punches and strikes are piston-like thrusts and their effectiveness is dependent on this relaxation. Some schools teach their students never to straighten the elbow out of fear of having an arm broken by an opponent. This is not a sound principle – according to Wing Chun ideas – because if the elbow remains bent there is still power to be released. In Wing Chun the elbow is straightened then returned to the position in Fig. 32, thus forming a triangle. Figs. 33/34 illustrate the principle of the triangle. In a later volume, the concept of the triangle will be developed in detail.

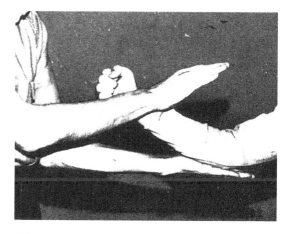

Fig. 32 shows side view. Fig. 33 a punch is thrown (right arrow) while defender tries an arm-breaking move. Fig. 34 shows counter move as punching arm is retracted to form a triangle.

In the beginning of your training you will experience some muscle soreness especially from the horse stance and the punches. The elbow joints will undoubtedly be painful. Use liniment and heat, and eventually the condition will pass. One way to minimize aching joints and muscles is to practise both "empty" and "solid" hitting. Empty punching involves practising before a mirror; as in shadow boxing you strike the air. This is very important for speed and form. But at least one third of the time and repetitions should be devoted to solid hitting against a sandbag mounted on the wall. Sandbags of this type can be purchased through any number of martial arts magazines. These bags can be filled with either dry peas or sand. Later on for variety you can try striking paper, a handkerchief, or a string hanging from the ceiling. The use of string is especially effective. It becomes the centreline. You punch at it without touching it.

In all exercises involving the alternate use of the hands, you generally begin with the left. The rationale for this is that since most people are right handed, one should start with the weakest hand. For variety we occasionally start with the right hand. Fig. 35. From basic position bring the right fist up to the middle of the chest, about four inches in front of it, palm facing the left and knuckles forward. Elbow close to body. Figs. 36.37 strike forward along the centreline until the elbow is straight. Your wrist should be straight at the completion of the punch. Fig. 38 bring the left hand forward over the right. Fig. 39 then execute an arrow punch with the left hand while retracting the right hand.

Note: the right hand should not be pulled back until the left hand is near it. The same applies to the left hand when you next throw a right arrow punch. Repeat for 20 reps. with each arm. The next day increase to 25 reps. per arm. Then continue increasing by 25 a day till you reach 300 with each arm.

Note: During training it is not necessary to tense your fists tightly. Remember that once the punch is completed the elbow should be relaxed again. Until you are sure of the form practise slowly. Gradually build up speed, but never sacrifice form for speed. Study the photographs carefully for proper extension and retraction of the arms. To relax your arms, do the umbrella exercise for 50 reps. each side, for each 100 reps. of the arrow punch.

Note: save for the umbrella, do not begin a new movement until you have reached the maximum number of reps. and sets for the arrow punch. This applies to all movements included in the book.

35

36

37

38

Umbrella

Although not a part of the Sil Lim Tao Form this relaxing exercise is a necessary part of training. Fig. 40. Maintain the pigeon-toed stance, but relax the muscles of the buttocks and straighten at the knees. Relax the body and let the arms hang naturally by the sides.

Fig. 41. Sing the hips and upper body to the left and to the right. The legs should remain stable and the arms relaxed. The momentum of the arms should carry the hips and upper body to each side, while the head moves along with the arms. Begin with 25 reps. to each side. This is the maximum to be done at any time.

CANDLE TEST

Fig. 42. After you reach 300 reps. in the arrow punch, attempt the candle test, which is an ancient Shaolin method for the demonstration of refined force. You will find this test mentioned throughout the book. Place a lighted candle in front of you at heart level. The candle should be a little over arm's length away from you so that your fist – or palm – is about 1 to 2 inches from the candle. Then deliver a punch. The speed of it should put out the candle. When you are able to do this, you can be sure that the punch or strike is effective. Note that it is important not to touch the candle.

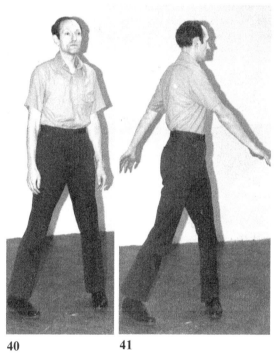

40　　　41

39

42

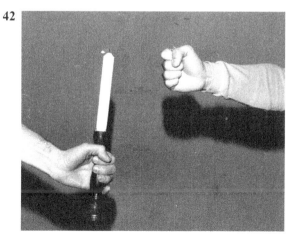

Open Hand Block

"Do you know the story of the praying mantis?" asked Chuang Tzu. "It raised its arm to stop an approaching carriage, unaware that this was beyond its power." Wing Chun never meets force with force. The open hand block, palm-up block, beggar hand block or palm-up hand (to mention some of its names) is a subtle, brilliant method of destroying the force of an opponent's blow without clashing with that force.

This block combines well with offensive moves and enables you to keep your hand inside an opponent's indoor area, thus leaving his vertical mid-line open to attack. See Fig. 43.

43

Exercises

Figs. 44, 45, 46. From the basic position extend the left hand forward until the elbow is about three inches from the body – about a fist's length from the body. The hand is open with the palm up, the elbow in, the forearm and hand pointing toward the centreline at heart level; i.e. the same position as inquisitive hand save that the palm is up. Return the arm to basic positin and repeat the movement with the right arm.

Perform this exercise slowly. Do 25 reps. with each hand. Work up to 100 reps. by increasing 25 reps. each day. When you do reach 100 reps do the umbrella exercise 25 reps.

44   Beginning of movement.

47

Side view.

Arrow Punch and Open Hand Block

Fig. 47. From the basic position deliver an arrow punch with the left hand while simultaneously executing an open hand block with the right hand. Then reverse the movements; i.e. retract the left hand into open hand block and extend right hand into arrow punch. Continue to do this alternately until you reach 25 reps. each hand. Increase daily by 25 until you reach 100 reps. Then umbrella exercise 25 reps. Then begin to increase daily by 25 reps. until you do another 100 reps. followed by 25 umbrella reps. Fig. 49 shows the application of this exercise

45   End of movement.

46   Completion of movement. Front view

48

49

17

Crossed Open Hand Block

The open hand block is normally applied to the inside of the opponent's attacking hand. In other words, the block places your hand within the opponent's indoor area. Thus, to stop a right hand punch, you would apply a left open hand block. You should not attempt to parry a roundhouse punch (hook) with an open hand

50

block until you have mastered the turning movements in level two (Chum Kil). There is in Wing Chun what is known as the crossed, open hand block in which you block the outside of the opponent's hand, i.e. you block a right with a right and a left with a left. This can be very effective when combined with a sideward palm punch, which will be introduced later. (See Fig. 50 for left hand open block against a left arrow).

Monkey Hand Block

Figs. 51/52.
This parry, also called the elbow in bent block, and the bridge-on-hand, is closely related to the circular wrist block. From the basic position extend the left hand until the elbow is about three inches in front of the body. The position is the

51

54

same as the open hand block, except that the hand is bent at the wrist and the back of the hand is facing forward with the palm facing you.

Fig. 53. Rotate the hand until the palm is facing down.

Fig. 54. Make into a fist and return to the basic position. Repeat with the right hand. Alternate the hands till you have done 20 reps. with each.

In application the monkey bridges the opponent's attacking hand. In executing the block, the arm must be relaxed and no strength applied. Later on, sparring exercises will be introduced which combine the monkey hand, the circular wrist block and the snake hand, with palm thrusts and other movements. Fig. 55 shows application.

52

53

55

Circular Wrist Block

While in the basic position execute an open hand block, Fig. 56. Rotate the hand until the palm faces the floor. Figs. 57/59. Make a fist and return to the basic position, Fig. 60. Then do the same with your right arm. Alternate the arms until you have done 20 reps. with each. Application: Fig. 61 - 'A' throws a left arrow punch while 'B' counters with a right circular wrist block. In sparring and self defence you never just execute a circular wrist block. Almost always the circular wrist block changes immediately into a sideward palm strike or a blow with the other hand as in Fig. 62. 'A' throws a left arrow punch, and 'B' counters with a crossed left circular wrist block and a right sideward palm strike.

56

57

59

60

58

61

62

Prayer Palm Block

This parry is also known as the slap block, but because the hands take a prayer-like position, the term "prayer palm block" is used. To get an idea of the prayer position, put the hands together as in the position of prayer, but thumbs are as in leaf palm, about three inches in front of the chest along the vertical mid-line. From the basic position, move the left hand into a prayer palm in front of the chest; then return to original position.

Figs. 63/64. Repeat the movement with the right hand, then the left, etc. Follow the same pattern of repetitions as the arrow punch with the umbrella between each 100 reps.

In application the prayer palm block may often go beyond the centreline, but under no circumstances should it go farther thn the shoulder, i.e. never beyond your own indoor area. Fig. 65.

Fig. 66/67 illustrate two applications. Fig. 66 'A' throws a left arrow punch into the heart of 'B'. 'B' counters simultaneously with a right prayer palm block and left arrow. Fig. 67 'A' throws a right arrow punch to the head of 'B' while 'B' parries it with a left prayer palm block and a right arrow punch at the same time.

63   **64**   **65**

66   **67**

SPARRING SETS

Arrow Punch and Prayer Palm

Fig. 68. Both begin in basic position. 'A' throws arrow punch with left, 'B' blocks with right prayer palm. Fig. 69. 'A' then strikes an arrow punch with right. 'B' parries with left hand prayer palm (right hand of 'B' remains in prayer palm position). Fig. 70. 'A' throws a left arrow punch which 'B' counters with a right prayer palm (remember the

left hand of 'B' remains in prayer palm position). Continue to alternate the hands for 50 reps. each hand. Relax for three minutes. Then do umbrella for 25 reps. Do two more sets of 50 reps. with the same rest pattern and umbrella sequence. You must be careful not to crowd each other in sparring. If you are too close together you cannot perform the movements properly. Notice the distance in the illustrations. Of course in all sparring sets, partners must switch about. One partner can be 'A' for one session and then 'B' for the next workout.

68

69

70

Arrow Punch, Open Hand Block and Prayer Palm

71

72

Fig. 71. Begin in basic position. 'A' throws arrow punch with left hand, while 'B' counters with a right open hand block and left arrow.

Fig. 72. 'A' blocks 'B' left arrow punch with a right prayer palm. Both return to basic position. For the second cycle 'A' begons with a right arrow punch which 'B' blocks with an open left hand and attacks with right arrow punch. 'A' in turn counters right arrow punch of 'B' with a left prayer palm. Follow the same repetition and rest pattern as the first sparring set.

VERTICAL PALM STRIKE

Vertical Palm Strike from Basic Position

73 74

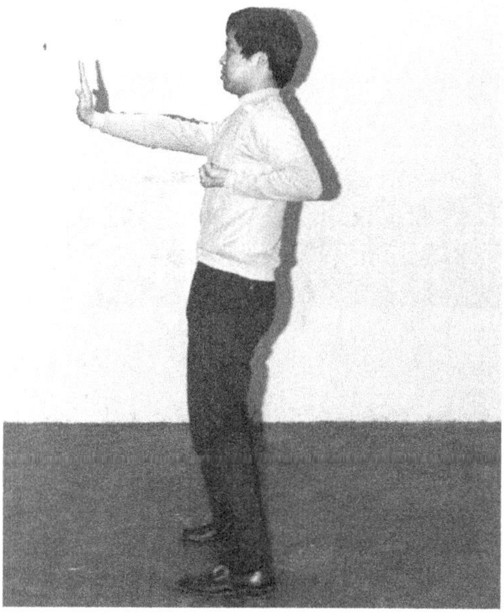

Figs. 73/74, Side view.

Fig. 73. Like other Wing Chun blows the vertical palm strike is a piston-like movement which depends upon speed and a relaxed elbow. From the basic position thrust the right hand, palm is vertical, forward along the centreline as in the arrow punch. Repeat with the left hand. Continue alternately for 25 reps. each hand. Increase by 25 daily, until you reach 100, each hand. Then, take the candle test.

Prayer Palm Block and Vertical Palm Strike

75

76

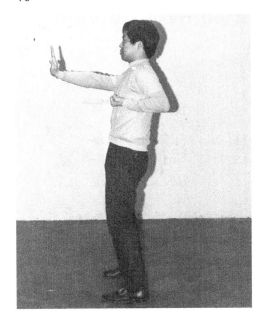

77

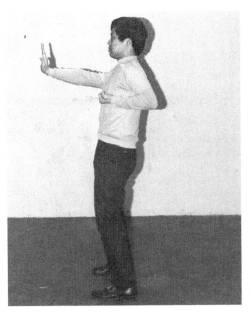

Figs. 75/77. Begin with left hand and execute a prayer palm block to the centreline and go immediately into a vertical palm strike. Return to the original position and repeat with right hand. Continue alternately for 25 reps. each hand. Increase by 25 each day until you reach 100. Work up to a total of 3 sets. 100 reps. each hand. Do the umbrella for 25 reps. after each set of 100. When you have reached the maximum number of sets, take the candle test.

Vertical Palm Strike
from Open Hand Block

78

79

Figs. 78/79. From the basic position move into an open hand block, left hand. Execute a vertical palm strike. Return to open hand block and do another vertical palm strike. Continue for 25 reps. before returning hand to basic position. Do the same with right hand. The reps. and sets are the same as those for the previous exercise, i.e. 3 sets of 100 reps. Take candle test when you have reached the maximum number of sets.

Sparring Set for Prayer Palm Block and Vertical Palm Strike

Figs. 80/81. 'A' executes a vertical palm strike with left hand while 'B' responds by countering with a right hand prayer palm block. 'A' delivers a vertical palm strike with right hand which 'B' blocks with a left hand prayer palm. Do alternately for 30 reps. each hand. Do 3 sets of 50 reps. After each set rest 3 minutes and do umbrella for 25 reps.

80

81

Push Down Palm

The following sequence of exercises is designed to develop the full range of the push down palm:

1. Left & right push down palm to side.
2. Double push down palm to rear, or back reverse palm.
3. Double push down palm in front.
4. Push down palm with one arrow punch, and
5. Push down palm with two arrow punches.

Remember that the push down palm is also a piston-like thrust.

82

83

84

85

Except for the back reverse palm, this sequence is only for practice. In sparring and self defence the fingers never face the front in executing a push down palm. The edge of the hand faces the opponent, otherwise you would break your fingers.

Figs. 82/83. From basic position push down left palm to side.

Figs. 84/85. Same for right hand.
Figs. 86/87. Then double push down, first bringing both hands behind back. Figs. 88/89.
Fig. 90. Raise hands and bring them in front of body. Palms are down.
Fig. 91. Execute a double push down, palm in front, then return hands to basic position.

Repeat the entire sequence for 50 reps.

86

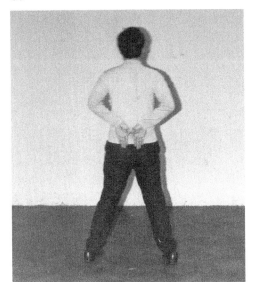

87

89

90

The push down palm can be either a block or a blow. As a parry it is effective against punches, strikes and kicks to the body. Fig. 92 illustrates how a single push down palm to the rear can be applied as a blow. 'B' grabs the right arm of 'A' from behind. 'A' counters with a back reverse palm. Top view in Fig. 93.

88

92

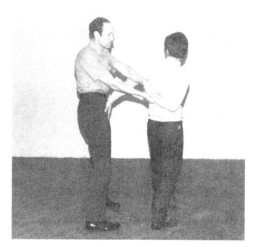

91

93

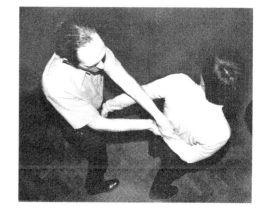

Push Down Palm with One Arrow Punch

Fig. 94/95. From basic position execute a left arrow punch and a right push down palm. Note that the edge of the hand faces forward in the push down palm. Fig. 96. Now raise right hand and strike an arrow punch while simultaneously executing a push down palm with the left. Continue for 25 reps. each hand. Increase by 25 reps. daily until you reach 100 reps. Then begin a second set in the same manner, i.e. 25 reps. a session to a maximum of 100 reps. followed by the umbrella 25 times. Fig. 97 shows the application of this exercise against a knee to the groin. 'A' attempts to drive left knee into groin area of 'B' but 'B' counters with a right push down palm and left arrow punch.

94

95

96

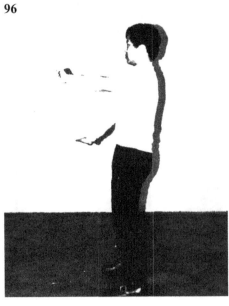

97

Push Down Palm with Two Arrow Punches

Fig. 98. From basic position execute an arrow punch with the left hand and a push down palm with the right. Fig. 99. Immediately raise right hand and strike an arrow punch while pulling left hand back to middle of chest in position to deliver another arrow punch. Now repeat the sequence by executing another right push down palm and a left arrow, etc. 25 reps.

Return to basic position. From this position strike an arrow punch with the right hand and a push down palm with the left. Immediately raise left and throw an arrow punch while pulling right hand back to centre of chest in position to deliver another arrow punch. Now repeat the sequence by executing a push down palm with the left hand while striking an arrow punch with the right, etc. 25 reps. Follow the same pattern for repetitions and sets as in the exercise for the push down palm with one arrow punch, i.e. 2 sets of 100 reps.

99

98

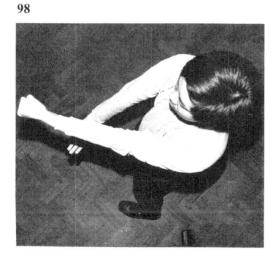

Sparring Set for Push Down Palm and Arrow Punch

Figs. 100/103. 'A' throws arrow punch with right hand, 'B' counters with left push down palm and right arrow punch. 'A' counters with left arrow punch going under right arrow of 'B'. 'B' withdraws right arrow and executes right push down palm while delivering a left arrow punch. 'A' simultaneously shoots right arrow punch under left of 'B'. Sequence begins again by 'B' withdrawing left arrow and executing a left push down palm and a right arrow punch, etc. 3 sets of 50 reps. for each arm.

This is only a practice sequence. In free sparring and self defence, you would not go under the opponent's forearm unless the forearm is away from the centreline. Remember the maxim: "When an opponent's forearm is coming, cross over it to punch." Fig. 104 illustrates this.

'A' throws a left arrow punch but 'B' counters by shooting a right arrow punch over the left arrow punch of 'A'.

100

101

102

103

104

EXTENDED HANDS

105

This movement is also called "spreading arms", "outside sweep" and "sweeping fingers". Fig. 105. From the basic position move the arms in front of the chest with palms down, left above right. Fig. 106. Shows half way position. Fig. 107. Simultaneously sweep both arms to position. Keep elbows relaxed. Return both arms to position in front of chest but this time with right above left. Extend arms again. 2 sets of 30 reps. Do 25 reps. of umbrella in between.

106

107

Application

The application of this movement in self defence is shown in Figs. 108a/108b/108c. 'A' is behind and rapidly grabs 'B' at shoulder. 'B' counters with a right extended hand to 'A' at the throat.

108a

108b

108c

Drop Elbow Block in Knife Hand Position

Drop Elbow Block from Extended Hand Position

Fig. 109. From basic position assume the opening position for extended hands movement with right hand over left. Fig. 110. Lower elbows so that forearms are parallel and palms are facing each other at the completion of the movement. Make sure that the elbows do not touch the body. Return to Fig. 109 position; 25 reps.

109

110

Drop Elbow Block from Basic Position

From basic position execute a drop elbow block with left arm. Return to original position. 25 reps. with each arm. Figs. 111/112.

Drop Elbow Block and Arrow Punch with same hand

Fig. 113. From basic position execute a drop elbow block with left arm. Fig. 114. Immediately strike an arrow punch with same arm.
Return to basic position. Repeat movements with right arm. Do 25 reps. each hand. Work up to 100, 25 increase daily. At 100 reps. do umbrella 25 times.

111

113

114

112

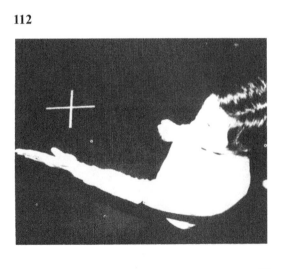

Drop Elbow Block and Arrow Punch with other hand

Fig. 115. From basic position execute a drop elbow block with left while simultaneously doing an arrow punch with right. Figs. 116a/116b. Lower right arm into drop elbow block while striking an arrow punch with left arm. Repeat sequence for 25 reps. Follow same repetition pattern as previous exercise.

115

116b

116a

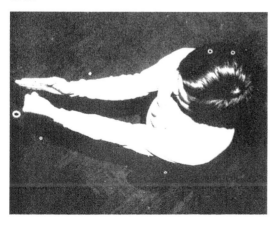

Drop Elbow Block
with Three Arrow
Punches

117

Fig. 117. Execute drop elbow block with both arms. Figs. 118a/118b. Then strike three rapid arrow punches – left, right, left. Return arms to basic position, and repeat for 25 reps. and work up to 100 as in the two previous exercises.

118b

118a

Drop Elbow Block and Yang Knife Hand to Throat

When the palm is down, the blow is called Yang Knife Hand. The Yin Knife Hand has been included in a later unit. The striking surface of the Yang Knife Hand is the edge of the hand and is delivered to the throat. See Fig. 119.

Fig. 120. From basic position execute a drop elbow block with left arm. Fig. 121. Immediately raise elbow till forearm is almost parallel to the floor with palm down; straighten arm to fullest extent. Do it in one fluid movement. Keep the elbow relaxed. Return arm to drop elbow position and repeat for 25 reps. Same for the right arm. Perform 3 sets of 50 reps. each arm. Figs. 122/123. Application. 'A' throws a right arrow punch; 'B' parries with left drop elbow. 'B' immediately moves from the drop elbow block into a Yang Knife Hand to throat of 'A'.

119

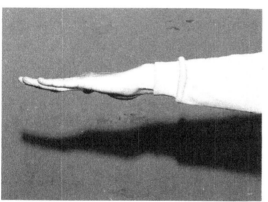

122

120   **121**

123

SPARRING SETS

Set One

Fig. 124. 'A' throws an arrow punch with the left hand. 'B' parries with a right drop elbow block. Fig. 125. 'B' immediately follows through with a right arrow punch, while 'A' defends with a left open hand block. Return to basic position. 'A' throws right arrow punch. 'B' counters with a left drop elbow block, etc. 3 sets of 50 reps. with 25 reps. umbrella movement between sets.

124

125

Set Two

Fig. 126. 'A' executes a left arrow punch. 'B' responds with right drop elbow block and left arrow punch. Fig. 127. 'A' defends with a right open hand block. Fig. 128. 'A' immediately changes the right open hand block into a a right vertical palm strike with 'B' parries with a left drop elbow block. Return to basic position. 'A' then throws right arrow punch. 'B' counters with left drop elbow block and right arrow punch, etc. 3 sets of 50 reps. with 25 reps. umbrella movement between sets.

126

127

128

Set Three

Fig. 129. 'A' executes a left vertical palm strike which 'B' blocks with right prayer palm. Fig. 130. 'B' immediately follows through with a right vertical palm strike. Fig. 131. 'A' counters with a left open hand block. Fig. 132. Then 'A' immediately executes a left palm strike, while 'B' parries with a right drop elbow block. Return to basic position. 'A' throws a right vertical palm strike which 'B' stops with a left prayer palm block, etc. 3 sets of 50 reps. with 25 umbrella reps. between.

129

130

131

132

Exercise Sequence for Snake Hand, Dart Fingers, Sliding Hand Block and Cannon Punch

Fig. 133. From basic position execute an open hand block with both hands. (In practice a double open hand block is done with forearms parallel.)

Fig. 134. Without moving the elbows turn palms away from you while jerking the hands slightly downwards (Jut Sao). Fig. 135. Then immediately thrust upwards with a dart fingers attack (Bil Jee). Fig. 136. Now push both palms down in front of body without bending the elbows (sliding hand block). Fig. 137. Raise arms up to shoulder level, fingers pointing downward. (This is a preliminary exercise for the cannon punch.) Return arms to basic position. Repeat sequence for 3 sets of 50 reps.

133

134

135

136

137

Snake Hand

Snake hand, also called 'shock hand', 'jerking hand' and 'retracting hand', is closely related to the monkey hand (Fook Sao). In fact it is quite easy to change from a monkey hand to a snake hand. The latter, a very effective surprise move, works best when the opponent's attacking hand is stiff. The idea is to press down the opponent's hand and retract. It will pull the opponent off balance and make him vulnerable to a dart fingers attack. The rapid way in which the hand is retracted and then thrust forward into the eyes has the appearance of a cobra strike.

138

139

140

SPARRING SET

Fig. 138. Side indoor where 'A' throws a left arrow punch which 'B' parries with right snake hand. 'A' throws right arrow and 'B' blocks with left snake hand. Continue for 2 sets of 50 reps. each hand – alternately. Fig. 139. Shows side outdoor. Fig. 140. Shows snake hand in self defence. 'A' throws a left arrow. 'B' countering simultaneously with snake hand, right, and a left arrow punch.

Dart Fingers

A 'dart fingers' thrust is delivered along the centreline into the eyes of an opponent. The execution of the movement involves three aspects: 1/ straightening the elbow 2/ power going into the wrist 3/ power going from wrist into the fingers which spread out as the thrust is delivered. See Fig. 141.

Fig. 142. 'A' throws arrow punch left. 'B' defends with left prayer palm and right dart fingers thrust.

Fig. 143. 'A' throws left arrow, parried by 'B' with right open hand block. Fig. 144. Open hand block of 'B' immediately changes into a dart fingers attack.

141

142

143

144

Fig. 145. 'A' throws arrow punch left. 'B' blocks with right snake hand. Fig. 146. 'B' changes his right snake into a dart fingers thrust, immediately.

Fig. 147. 'A' throws a right arrow punch which 'B' blocks with a left snake hand. Fig. 148. 'B' straight away uses right protective hand to chop the right hand of 'A' aside while simultaneously executing a dart fingers thrust with left hand.

145

146

147

148

Sliding Hand Block

This block is an excellent defence against a straight punch along your centreline. The block throws your opponent off balance by drawing him forward, thus making him vulnerable to any counter attack. It is done by sliding palm down your opponent's arm without bending the elbow. Sometimes this block can be used as a vertical palm strike, but this type of attack involves forward motion which is part of the second level Wing Chun. Figs. 149/150. 'A' throws a left arrow. 'B' blocks with a sliding hand block.

149

150

Sliding Hand Block Exercise

151

152

153

Fig. 151. From basic position move right hand straight in front. Fig. 152. Execute a right sliding hand block and a left arrow punch. Fig. 153. Drop left into a sliding hand block while right becomes an arrow punch. Do alternately for 3 sets of 50 reps. each hand. Increase by 25 reps. daily, until you reach 100 reps. for each set.

Sliding Hand Block Sparring Set

Fig. 154. 'A' throws a right arrow punch. 'B' parries with a left sliding hand block while simultaneously executing a right arrow punch. Fig. 155. 'A' counters with a left sliding hand block while retracting right hand and then striking a right arrow. The sequence re-commences. 2 sets of 50 reps.

154

156

155

Application

Fig. 156. 'A' throws a left arrow punch, 'B' countering with a right sliding hand block and a left dart fingers thrust.

Cannon Punch

Sometimes our hands will be at your sides and you must do a rapid arrow punch from that position. This movement is called a 'cannon punch'.

Exercise

Fig. 157/159. From basic position move left hand down in front of body. Elbow should be relaxed. Raise the arm up the centreline while executing an arrow punch to the mouth level of an imaginary opponent. Continue for 50 reps. then do 50 reps. with the right arm. Do 2 sets of 50 reps. with each arm. Increase by 25 reps. daily until you reach 100 reps. for each set.

157

158

159

160

Application

Fig. 160. 'A' throws an arrow punch left. 'B' counters with a right cannon punch penetrating 'A' indoor area.

Thrusting Block

There are two types of thrusting block. One with palm facing to the side, the other with the palm facing downward. Thrusting blocks are effective against high punches. In executing these blocks you thrust upward from your centreline. See Fig. 161. Figs. 162/163 illustrate these two types of block. Fig. 162. 'A' throws a right arrow punch. 'B' parries with a left thrusting block palm down. Fig. 163. 'A' throws a right arrow punch which 'B' counters with a left thrusting block with palm to side.

161

162

163

Sideward Palm Strike, Downward Palm Strike, and Yin Knife Hand

There are two types of sideward palm strikes. One is to the chest and the other is to the ribs. When one strikes the chest the power is concentrated in the heel of the palm. See Fig. 164. When the target is the ribs, power is concentrated in the edge of the hand. See Fig. 165.

In Kung Fu it is believed that human spiritual forces (Ch'i) are released from the lower abdominal area about three inches below the navel, and this region is called the Tan Tien. The downward palm strike is directed to the Tan Tien area. The power is centred in the heel of the palm. See Fig. 166. Although all palm strikes, in Wing Chun, are considered Yin, the final one under discussion bears the name 'Yin knife hand'. It is delivered to the neck, and the power is concentrated in the edge of the hand. See Fig. 167.

164   **165**   **166**   **167**

Exercise for Sideward Palm Strike to Chest

Fig. 168. From basic position move left hand into prayer palm position at the centreline. Fig. 169. Do a Sideward palm strike along the centreline. For this sequence the arm should be parallel with the floor. Here also as in the palm strikes described keep the elbow relaxed. Fig. 170. The heel of the palm should strike the centreline of the opponent's chest. Figs. 171/172. After completing the sideward palm strike to the chest, execute a circular wrist movement. Figs. 173. Then clench fist and return arm to basic position. Then repeat for 25 reps. left arm. Same for right arm. In all do a total of 3 sets of 25 reps. each arm.

168   **169**   **170**

171   **172**   **173**

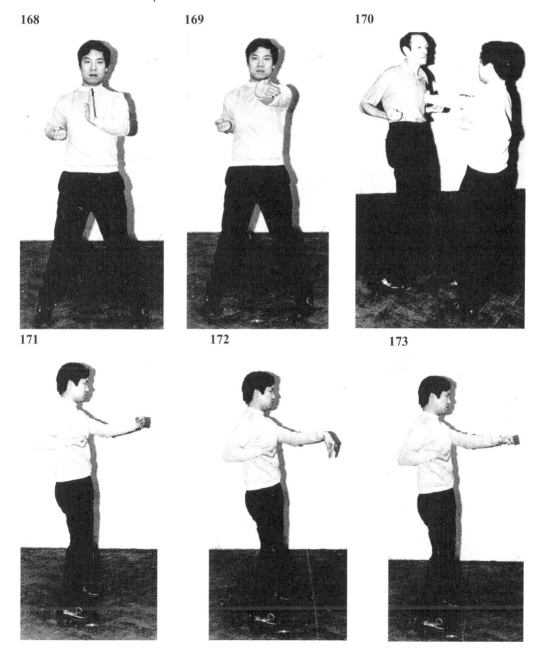

Exercise for Sideward Palm Strike to Ribs

Fig. 174. From basic position move left hand into prayer palm position at centreline. Then execute a sideward palm strike to the ribs of an imaginary opponent. As in the previous exercise, end with a circular wrist movement, clench fist and return arm to basic position. Repeat 25 times and then perform exercise with the right arm. As in the previous exercise, do three sets of 25 reps. each arm. Fig. 175 shows application of the strike.

Exercise for Downward Palm Strike to Tan Tien

Fig. 176. From basic position execute an open hand block with left hand. Thrust arm forward along centreline while moving fingers downward. In training the arm is thrust straight forward so that the arm is parallel with floor. This will build your power but I application the strike is to the Tan Tien. Remember that the heel of the palm is up and the main force of the strike is centred in the heel of the palm. Return to open hand block position and repeat for 25 reps. before assuming the basic position. Then switch to the right arm for 25 reps. Continue until you have completed 3 sets of 25 reps. with each arm. Fig. 177 shows its application.

174

176

175

177

Exercise for Yin Knife Hand to Neck

Fig. 178. From basic position thrust left hand straight forward along centreline. Remember that the striking surface is the edge of the hand. Fig. 179. Retract left hand to prayer palm position as the right hand thrusts forward along the centreline. Return right hand to the prayer palm position as left is thrust forward. Continue to strike alternately for 3 sets of 25 reps. each arm. Fig. 180 shows application of this strike.

Try the candle test with each of these strikes. The striking surface will be either the heel of the palm or the edge of the hand. The latter strike is especially difficult and considerable practice may be necessary before you can extinguish the candle.

178

179

180

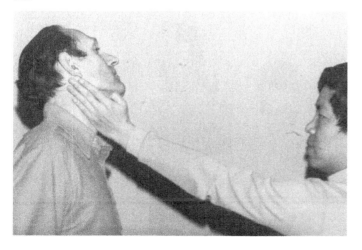

SPARRING SETS

Fig. 181. 'A' throws an arrow punch with the left hand which 'B' counters with a right monkey hand into a circular wristblock. Fig. 182. In Fig. 183 'B' follows his circular wrist block by a sideward palm strike to 'A' in the ribs. (On the second set use a downward palm strike to the Tan Tien instead of sideward palm strike). See Fig. 184. 'B' executes downward palm strike to Tan

Tien. Figs. 185/186. 'A' responds with a left arrow punch. In fact 'A' merely has to retract is arm slightly and move around 'B's arm in order to get it in position for arrow punch. This method of slipping a block is called a 'running hand'. It follows the maxim of following the body and not the hand. Fig. 187. 'B' in turn counters with a right open hand block. 50 reps. Switch to other hand, i.e. 'A' begins by throwing arrow punch with right hand. Do a total of 3 sets of 50 reps. with each arm.

181

183

182

184

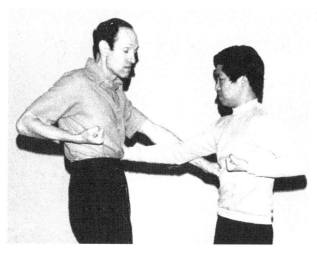

185

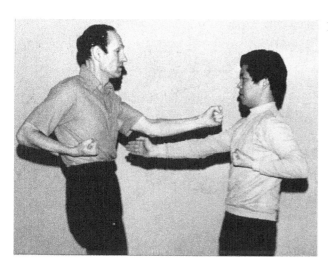

186

187

Sparring Set – Two

Fig. 188. 'A' throws a left arrow punch. 'B' parries with a right push down palm while simultaneously striking a left Yin knife hand to the neck of 'A'. Fig. 189. 'A' counters with a right thrusting block. Return arms to basic. 'A' then throws a right arrow punch and the sequence continues. Repeat alternately for 25 reps. Do 3 sets of 25 reps. with each hand.

188

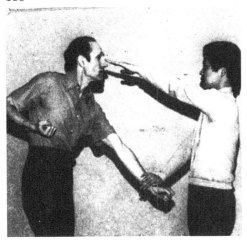

189

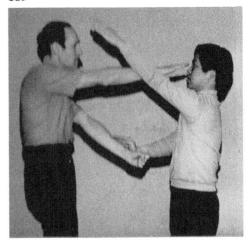

Application

As in all the applications illustrated in this book, we have only chosen a few. There is no rigid pattern in Wing Chun. The combinations are endless. You must respond instinctively and not on the basis of certain memorized movements. Fig. 190. 'A' throws right arrow. 'B' counters with crossed right open hand block and a left sideward palm strike to the ribs of 'A'. Fig. 191. 'A' attempts a double punch which 'B' parries with a crossed right open hand block and a left sideward palm strike to the ribs. In Fig. 192 'A' throws left arrow. 'B' counters with right open hand block. Fig. 193. From the right open hand block 'B' immediately strikes a Yin knife hand to the neck of 'A'.

190

191

192

193

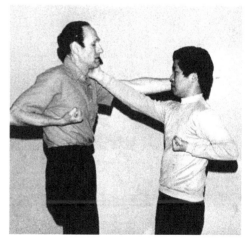

CULTIVATING HAND BLOCK

This movement, which resembles someone cultivating the land, i.e. sowing seed, is used to block blows and kicks to the middle area. The entire surface of the arm from elbow to finger tips is the blocking area. See Fig. 194. Shows the surface area for cultivating hand block.

LINED AREA IS USED FOR BLOCKING. 50 reps.

Exercise – Cultivating Hand from Basic Position

Fig. 195. From basic position do an open hand block with left hand. Fig. 196/197. Immediately chop hard downward without moving the position of the elbow. Return to open hand block position and from there back to basic position. Then execute the movements with the right hand. Do alternately for 25 reps. First, perform the movements slowly to be certain that you are doing them properly. Make sure that the completed cultivating hand does not go beyond the indoor area. Each day increase by 25 reps. until you reach 100 reps. with each hand. Then do umbrella 25 times.

195

194

196

197

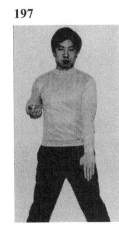

Exercise – Cultivating Hand from Open Hand Block

From basic position do an open hand block with left hand. Execute a cultivating hand. Return to an open hand block position and repeat for 25 reps. Do the same with the right hand. Follow the same pattern for reps. and sets as in the previous exercise.

Sparring Set – One

Fig. 198. 'A' throws left arrow punch to upper chest of 'B'. 'B' parries with a right open hand block. Fig. 199. 'A' executes a running hand, i.e. lowers left arm and attempts another arrow punch to ribs of 'B'. 'B' counters with a right cultivating hand. Return to basic position. 'A' ten throws a right arrow punch which 'B' counters with a left open hand, etc. Do alternately for 3 sets of 50 reps. each hand.

198

199

Exercise – Arrow Punch and Cultivating Hand

Fig. 200. From basic position simultaneously execute a left arrow punch and a right cultivating hand. Fig. 201. Drop left into a cultivating hand while raising right into an arrow. Do alternately for 25 reps. each hand. Increase by 25 reps. each day until you reach 100 reps. Then do umbrella 25 times. Work up to a second set of 100 reps. with umbrella after it.

Exercise – Arrow Punch and Open Hand Block

Fig. 202. From basic position simultaneously execute a left arrow punch and a right open hand lock. Fig. 203. Immediately lower the left arm into a cultivating hand and change the right open hand block into an arrow punch. Fig. 204. Raise left cultivating hand into an arrow punch, while you lower right arrow into an open hand block.

200

201

Fig. 205. Lower left arrow into an open hand block while simultaneously raising right open hand block into an arrow punch. Fig. 206. Raise left open hand block into an arrow, while you lower right arrow into a cultivating hand. Fig. 207. Raise right cultivating hand into an arrow while you lower left arrow into an open hand block. Then lower right arrow into an open hand block and simultaneously raise left open hand block into an arrow punch. You are now ready to do the sequence as in Fig. 202. Perform the exercise sequence slowly for 3 sets of 50 reps. After each set rest three minutes and do the umbrella 25 times.

202　　　　　**203**　　　　　**204**

205　　　　　**206**　　　　　**207**

Sparring Set – Two

Fig. 208. 'A' delivers left arrow which 'B' parries with a right open hand block, while simultaneously striking with a left arrow punch. Return to basic position. Fig. 209. 'A' then does a right arrow which 'B' parries with a left open hand block while striking with a right arrow punch. Return to basic position. Do alternately for 50 reps. Follow same repetition and set pattern as the previous exercise, i.e. 3 sets of 50 reps. 3 minute rests and umbrella.

Sparring Set – Three

Fig. 210. 'A' does a left arrow punch. 'B' responds with a right open hand block and left arrow punch. Fig. 211. 'A' delivers a right arrow punch under the left arrow punch of 'B', but 'B' counters by blocking with a left cultivating hand and right arrow punch.

Return to basic position. 'A' then does a right arrow punch. 'B' responds with a left open hand block and a right arrow punch. 'A' then delivers a left arrow punch under right arrow of 'B', but 'B' counters by blocking with right cultivating hand and left arrow punch. 3 sets of 50 reps. Follow the same rep. and set pattern as in the sparring set no. 2.

208

210

209

211

Application

Since the sparring sets provide examples of
application of the cultivating hand, only a single
illustration is given here, i.e. as a block to a kick.
Fig. 212. 'A' kicks with right leg and 'B' parries
with left cultivating hand.

212

WING HAND BLOCK

The wing hand or elbow-up-block is one of the most effective and versatile parries. It is also the most difficult to execute. For this reason Yip Man said that the wing hand was the best or the worst of movements. If it cannot be done properly, then it should not be done at all. "The soft and weak can overcome the hard and strong. Blunt all that is sharp." So said Lao-Tsu. The wing hand which looks so fragile can dissipate the force of even the most powerful punch. The passive nature of this parry has been compared to a piece of timber floating on the water. If you press evenly in the centre, the timber will submerge. But if you press on one end of it, the timber will merely yield, tilt, discharge your arm's weight and return to its original position.

In actual fighting you never execute a wing hand without a protective hand. Fig. 213. In addition, it is always accompanied by a punch in which the protective hand chops away the opponent's arm, and the wing then converts into an arrow punch or a Yang Knife Hand. Or, if there is no punch, the wing is used in conjunction with a push as you move forward. This latter move will be introduced in level two.

In executing the wing hand, the elbow must go up first. The arm is at an angle, with hand, wrist, and fingers relaxed. The elbow is pointing up, while the fingers are pointing down. See Figs. 214/215. The slope and angle of the arm allows for the greatest possible surface of contact with which to deflect an opponent's arm. Figs. 216/217. The wing hand can be used against any straight punch but generally not against a roundhouse swing. In general it is more effective against a punch not higher than the chest. In addition, your blocking hand must be below your opponent's attacking hand. There are some variations such as the crossed wing hand and the low wing hand which are illustrated later in this book.

213

214

215

Exercise – Wing Hand from Basic Position

Fig. 218. From basic position execute a wing hand with left hand. Return to basic position. Repeat with left hand 50 times. Then 50 reps. with right hand. Perform 3 sets of 50 reps. with each arm. Look carefully at the photographs of the wing hand and watch your position in a mirror.

216

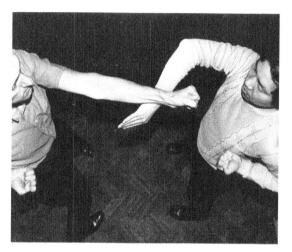

218

217

Exercise – Wing Hand, Open Hand Block

Sparring Set – One

219   **220**   **221**

222

From basic position do a left wing hand as in Fig. 218. Fig. 219. Lower your elbow to an open hand block position. Fig. 220. Then perform a vertical palm strike. Return to left wing hand. Do 50 reps. with left hand; 50 reps. with right. Do 3 sets of 50 reps. each arm.

Fig. 221. 'A' throws left arrow. 'B' parries with right drop elbow block. Fig. 222. 'B' immediately follows up with a right Yang knife hand to 'A's throat, but 'A' blocks with a left wing hand. Continue for 50 reps. followed by the umbrella 25 times. Do a total of 3 sets of 50 reps. each arm with 25 reps. of umbrella between sets.

Sparring Set – Two

Fig. 223. 'A' throws left arrow punch. 'B' blocks with right wing hand. Fig. 224. 'B' quickly shifts into a right open hand block position. Fig. 225. 'B' immediately strikes a right vertical strike which 'A' parries with a left drop elbow block. As in Fig. 223. 'A' follows with a left arrow punch with 'B' blocks with a right wing hand. Continue the sequence for 50 reps. followed by the umbrella for 25 reps. 'A' then throws a right arrow. 'B' blocks with a left wing hand, etc. 50 reps. and umbrella for 25 reps. Performa total of 3 sets of 50 reps. each arm with 25 reps. of umbrella in between sets.

223

224

225

Exercise – Wing Hand and Protective Hand Combination

Fig. 226. From basic position execute a left wing and a right protective hand. Note the position of the protective hand. Fig. 227. Move right protective hand outward and change it to a wing hand, while the left wing hand moves inward and changes into a protective hand. Do alternately for 3 sets of 50 reps.

226

227

Application

Fig. 228. 'A' throws a left arrow punch. 'B' blocks with a right wing hand while simultaneously raising the left into a protective hand position. Figs. 229/230. 'B' uses left protective hand to chop 'A's left arrow hand aside while simultaneously change the right wing into an arrow punch.

228

229

230

LAP SAO

This sparring set is called "Lap Sao" or "Warding Off Hands" and is a classic Wing Chun exercise. Fig. 231. Begin in basic position. 'A' throws arrow punch with left hand while moving right into protective hand position. 'B' parries with right wing hand while moving left into high protective hand position. Fig. 232. 'A' uses right protective hand to push 'B's right wing forward. 'B uses left protective hand to chop 'A's left arrow hand aside.

Fig. 233. 'B' changes right wing hand into a right arrow punch, but 'A' counters with a left wing hand which 'B' pushes with left protective hand. 'A' then uses right protective hand to chop 'B's right arrow hand aside, while changing left wing hand into an arrow punch. The new cycle continues with 'B' countering with a right wing hand, etc. Then return to basic.

'A' throws an arrow punch with right hand while moving left into protective hand position. 'B' parries with left wing hand while moving right into high protective hand position. 'A' uses left protective hand to push 'B's left wing hand forward. 'B' uses right protective hand to chop 'A's right arrow hand aside. 'B' changes left wing hand into a left arrow punch, but 'A' counters with a right wing hand which 'B' pushes with right protective hand. 'A' then uses left protective hand to chop 'B's left arrow hand aside while changing right wing hand into an arrow punch. The new cycle continues with 'B' countering with a left wing hand, etc. Each cycle counts for one rep. Do 50 times.

231

232

233

WING HAND VARIATIONS

Low Wing Hand Block

Fig. 234. 'A' throws a left arrow punch to the stomach of 'B'. 'B' parries with a right low wing hand.

234

Crossed Wing Hand, Open Hand Block and Sideward Palm Strike Combination

Fig. 235. 'A' throws a right arrow punch which 'B' parries with a crossed right wing hand.

235

236

Fig. 236. 'B' changes from a right wing hand into a right open hand block while executing a left sideward palm strike to the ribs of 'A'.

Crossed Wing Hand, Snake Hand and Yang Knife Combination

Fig. 237. 'A' throws left arrow punch. 'B' counters with a crossed left wing hand with right held in protective hand position. Fig. 238. 'B' then shifts to a left snake hand while executing a right Yang knife hand to neck of 'A'.

237

238

Downward Sweep and Chop

Application

Fig. 239. From basic position move left arm down and slant it across the body as shown; keep the wrist straight. Bring the right hand across the chest, palm facing up as shown; keep the wrist straight. Fig. 240. Slide the right hand down while bringing the left up. As you near the end of the downward sweep with the right hand the palm should turn towards your body so that you end with a chopping motion. When the movement is completed the hands are in reverse position. Now slide the left hand down while bring the right up, etc. Do the movements rapidly. Do 2 sets of 50 reps. with each hand.

Fig. 241. 'A' grabs right wrist of 'B'. Fig. 242. 'B' executes a downward sweep and chop. Fig. 243. 'B' strikes a right arrow punch immediately after 'A's grip has been released as a result of the chop. It must be one rapid movement.

239   **240**

241   **242**   **243**

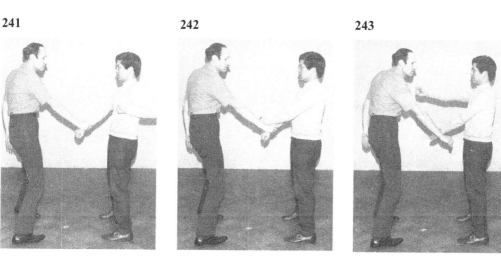

Sticking Hands

"If the other moves slightly, then the self moves sooner than he" (Wang Chung-Yueh). This basic maxim from Tai Chi Chuan best summarizes the two-fold purpose of this classic Wing Chun sparring set, i.e. sensitivity and speed. These movements, called "sticking hands", are unique to Wing Chun. They incorporate six movements: 1/ open hand block 2/ monkey hand 3/ vertical palm strike 4/ snake hand 5/ arrow punch 6/ wing hand. Throughout this sparring set the arms touch and there is no attempt to actually hurt one another.

Fig. 244. 'A' and 'B' face each other in the basic position. 'A' extends left arm in open hand block. 'B' puts his right arm over 'B's arm in monkey hand position. Fig. 245. 'A' attempts left vertical palm. 'B' "feels" the move and parries with a right snake hand. Fig. 246. shows a variation. Here 'B' counters with a right drop elbow block. Fig. 247. From the snake hand (or drop elbow block) 'B' attempts a right arrow punch, but 'A' "feels" the movement and counters with a left wing hand. 'A' and 'B' return to the original position as in Fig. 244. Repeat for 50 reps. Then shift to the other arm. 'A' extends right arm in open hand block, while 'B' puts left monkey hand over 'B's arm, etc. Repeat sequence for 50 times also. 2 sets of 50 reps. each arm.

244

245

246

247

THE SIL LIM TAO SET

(The movements of the Sil Lim Tao Set which follow have been described in some detail in the preceding chapters; so no detailed description will be given in the presentation of the Set which follows.)

In a number of systems, students memorise and practice numerous fist sets, etc., often without knowing the meaning of the movements. Also, students often find it difficult to apply the individual and, at times, stylized forms, apart from the entire sequence. In Wing Chun each punch, strike, thrust and block is practiced separately until one can respond instinctively. The Sil Lim Tao only becomes relevant once the application of each movement is understood. Then, the Set becomes a useful training device. In fact each workout should then begin with Sil Lim Tao.

Now that you are familiar with all the movements, less description is necessary, but there are abundant pictures to assist you in mastering the subtle moves. In order to facilitate the learning process and to ease the burden on your memory, we have divided the Set into 14 sections. Remember that you remain stationary while performing the entire sequence. The attacking movements (all punches, strikes and thrusts) should be done rapidly. Defensive moves should be executed slowly, save those blocks which can also be used to attack, e.g. push down palm and cultivating hand. These latter movements should also be done rapidly.

We believe this book to be the most complete and systematic treatment of Wing Chun thus far in print in any language. Your success will depend to a great extent upon your own determination and discipline.

There is a Chinese proverb to the effect that one can always find a higher mountain. Master Yip disagreed for he told his students: "If you stand on the highest mountain, there is none higher. Wing Chun is the highest."

There is no better conclusion we could think of than the advice of Chuang Tsu: "Listen with your vital energy (chi). It is receptive to all things. Leave no opening. And you will not be harmed. Be always at one and accept whatever happens. Then you are close to success."

SIL LIM TAO

1. Entering the Horse Stance. S. 1-4.
2. Double Cultivating Hand. S. 5-7.
3. Left Hand: Arrow Punch and Circular Wrist Block: 8-14.
4. Right Hand: Same movements as no. 3. S 15-21.
5. Left Hand: Open Hand Block, Circular Wrist Block, Prayer Palm (away from and near body at centreline). Kowtow three times, Prayer Palm (to shoulder and centreline), Vertical Palm Strike, Circular Wrist Block. S. 22-38.
6. Right Hand: Same movements as no. 5. S. 39-55.
7. Both Hands: Push Down Palm (left, right, back, reverse, in front), Extended Hands, Double drop Elbow Block, Double Open Hand Block, Snake Hand, Dart Fingers, Sliding Hand Block, Cannon Punch Exercise. S. 56-71.
8. Left Hand: Prayer Palm (to shoulder and to centreline), Sideward Palm Strike to Chest (or Yin Knife Hand), Circular Wrist Block. S. 72-78.

1

2

9. Right Hand: Same movements as no. 8. S.79-85.
10. Left Hand: Open Hand Block, Cultivating Hand, Open Hand Block, Circular Wrist Block, Sideward Palm Strike to Ribs, Circular Wrist Block. S. 86-94.
11. Right Hand: Same movements as no. 10. S. 95-103.
12. Left Hand: Wing Hand, Open Hand Block, Downward Palm Strike, Circular Wrist Block. S. 104-110.
13. Right Hand: Same movements as no. 12. S. 111-117.
14. Both Hands: Downward Sweep and Chop (right, left, right), Arrow Punch (left, right, left). S. 118-125.
    KOWTOW: this series of movements consists of a combination of Monkey Hand, ahile moving hand forward along centreline, Open hand block, Circular wrist, Prayer palm (away from and near the body at the centreline) and it is repeated 3 times.

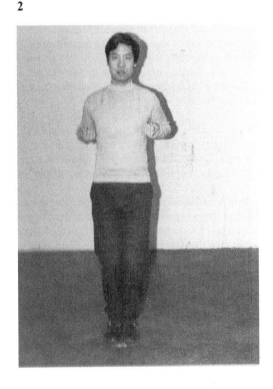

3

4

5

6

7

8

9

10

11

12

13

14

15

16

17

18

19

20

21

22

23

24

25

26

27

28

29

30

31

32

33

34

NOTE: The circular wrist block begins from the palm up position after the vertical palm strike in Fig. 34.

88

35

36

37

38

39

40

41

42

90

43

44

45

46

47

48

49

50

51

52

53

54

55

56

57

Photo 58 shows the move following 57. It is performed facing the same direction.

58

59

60

61

95

62

63

64

65

66

67

68

69

70

71

72

73

74

75

76

77

78

79

80

81

82

83

84

85

86

87

88

89

90

91

92

93

94

95

96

97

98

99

100

101

102

103

104

105

106

107

108

109

110

111

112

113

114

115

116

117

118

119

120

121

122

123

124

111

Lightning Source UK Ltd.
Milton Keynes UK
UKOW06f2058110714

234996UK00001B/3/P